POEMS
5 YEAR OLDS

Susie Gibbs has worked in the world of children's poetry for eleven years. Her many nephews, nieces and godchildren were invaluable testing grounds for *Poems for 5 Year Olds*, and she very much hopes that they and their friends will enjoy this book. Susie lives aboard her narrowboat, *Hesperus II*, with one husband, no pets but plenty of wildlife.

Liane Payne was born in 1963 and trained to be a fine artist at Norwich School of Art. On graduating, she soon discovered that life in a lonely garret wasn't for her, and working as an illustrator was much more interesting and fun!

Also available from Macmillan Children's Books

POEMS FOR 6 YEAR OLDS
Chosen by Susie Gibbs

POEMS FOR 7 YEAR OLDS
Chosen by Susie Gibbs

POEMS FOR 8 YEAR OLDS
Chosen by Susie Gibbs

POEMS FOR 9 YEAR OLDS
Chosen by Susie Gibbs

POEMS FOR 10 YEAR OLDS
Chosen by Susie Gibbs

POEMS FOR 5 YEAR OLDS

CHOSEN BY
Susie Gibbs

ILLUSTRATED BY
Liane Payne

MACMILLAN CHILDREN'S BOOKS

*Dedicated with love to all my godchildren:
Rufus, Harry, George, Clare, George, Sam
and Anoushka.*

First published 2000
by Macmillan Children's Books
a division of Macmillan Publishers Ltd
25 Eccleston Place, London SW1W 9NF
Basingstoke and Oxford
www.macmillan.com

Associated companies throughout the world

ISBN 0 330 48303 X

This collection copyright © Susie Gibbs 2000
Illustrations copyright © Liane Payne 2000

The right of Susie Gibbs to be identified as the
author of this book has been asserted by her in accordance
with the Copyright, Designs and Patents Act 1988.

All rights reserved. No part of this publication may be
reproduced, stored in or introduced into a retrieval system, or
transmitted, in any form, or by any means (electronic, mechanical,
photocopying, recording or otherwise) without the prior written
permission of the publisher. Any person who does any unauthorized act
in relation to this publication may be liable to criminal prosecution and
civil claims for damages.

1 3 5 7 9 8 6 4 2

A CIP catalogue record for this book is available from the British Library.

Printed by Mackays of Chatham plc, Chatham, Kent.

This book is sold subject to the condition that it shall not,
by way of trade or otherwise, be lent, re-sold, hired out,
or otherwise circulated without the publisher's prior consent
in any form of binding or cover other than that in
which it is published and without a similar condition including
this condition being imposed on the subsequent purchaser.

Contents

Ode to an Extinct Dinosaur – *Doug MacLeod*	1
Over in the Meadow – *Anon*	2
As Soon as Fred Gets Out of Bed – *Jack Prelutsky*	6
Ice Lolly – *Pie Corbett*	7
As I Went Down Zig Zag – *Charles Causley*	8
Moses – *Anon*	11
Round the Rugged Rock – *Anon*	11
Five Little Chickens – *Anon*	12
Tailor – *Eleanor Farjeon*	14
Two Witches – *Alexander Resnikoff*	16
My Heterodontosaurus – *Leon Rosselson*	17
Learner – *Anon*	21
My Daddy Dances Tapstep – *Peter Dixon*	22
I Thought ... – *John Foster*	23
The Three Little Kittens – *Eliza Lee Follen*	24
Bedtime – *Eleanor Farjeon*	27
I Am a Ghost Who's Lost His Boo – *Jack Prelutsky*	28
Chums – *Arthur Guiterman*	30
A Frog He Would A-Wooing Go – *Anon*	31
The Furry Ones – *Aileen Fisher*	35
The Cupboard – *Walter de la Mare*	36
As I Was Going to St Ives – *Anon*	38
Finger-nails – *Anon*	39
Wynken, Blynken, and Nod – *Eugene Field*	40

Mice – *Miles Gibson*	43
Deborah Delora – *Anon*	43
The Owl and the Pussy-Cat – *Edward Lear*	44
Cow – *Ted Hughes*	46
Ready for Spaghetti – *Peggy Guthart*	47
The Mouse, the Frog and the Little Red Hen – *Anon*	48
Where Are You Going To? – *Anon*	50
Toes in My Nose – *Sheree Fitch*	51
Five Little Monkeys – *Anon*	52
Mumbling Bees – *Daphne Lister*	53
The North Wind Doth Blow – *Anon*	54
A Rabbit Raced a Turtle – *Anon*	57
Riddle – *Judith Nicholls*	58
One, Two, Three, Four, Five – *Anon*	59
Mother Duck – *Anon*	60
The Picnic – *Dorothy Aldis*	61
How to be Angry – *Eve Merriam*	62
Sneezing – *Anon*	63
There was a Young Girl – *Anon*	63
Jelly Jake and Butter Bill – *Leroy F. Jackson*	64
Maggie – *Anon*	65
The Cat's Pyjamas – *Irene Rawnsley*	66
The Elf and the Dormouse – *Oliver Herford*	68
Bath Time – *Eve Merriam*	70
Simple Simon – *Anon*	72
Three Ghostesses – *Anon*	73
The Clucking Hen – *Anon*	74
Pease Porridge – *Anon*	75

Captain Conniption – *Jack Prelutsky*	76
Muddy Boots – *Philip Paddon*	78
Mr Finney's Turnip – *Anon*	80
Granny, Granny, Please Comb My Hair – *Grace Nichols*	82
Night, Knight – *Anon*	83
My Gran – *Moira Andrew*	84
Give Me a House – *Charles Causley*	86
There was a Little Girl – *Anon*	87
The Gingerbread Man – *Rowena Bennett*	88
Breakfast for One – *Judith Nicholls*	90
Be Kind to Dumb Animals – *John Ciardi*	91
What I'll Do To Make You Laugh – *Jeff Moss*	91
I'm Not Frightened of Pussy Cats – *Spike Milligan*	92
My Name Is – *Pauline Clarke*	93
Little Bo-Peep – *Anon*	94
Not a Very Cheerful Song, I'm Afraid – *Adrian Mitchell*	95
Grandma's Lullaby – *Charlotte Pomerantz*	96
Tiger, Tiger – *Pam Ayres*	97
Countdown – *Jack Prelutsky*	98
Bears Don't Like Bananas – *John Rice*	99
I Speak, I Say, I Talk – *Arnold L. Shapiro*	100
My Brother is as Generous as Anyone Could Be – *Jack Prelutsky*	102
I've Never Seen the Milkman – *Charles Causley*	104
Hickory, Dickory, Dock – *Anon*	106
Wild Beasts – *Evaleen Stein*	107

Through the Teeth – *Anon*	108
Clatter – *Joyce Armor*	109
Quack, Quack! – *Dr Seuss*	110
be be be quiet – *Mark Warren*	111
A Cough – *Robert Graves*	111
Some Things Don't Make Any Sense At All – *Judith Viorst*	112
The Pancake – *Christina Rossetti*	113
The Mouse – *Elizabeth Coatsworth*	114
Monday's Child – *Anon*	115
Rolling Down a Hill – *Colin West*	116
A Wise Old Owl – *Anon*	118
Acknowledgements	119

Ode to an Extinct Dinosaur

Iguanodon, I loved you,
With all your spiky scales,
Your massive jaws,
Impressive claws
And teeth like horseshoe nails.

Iguanodon, I loved you.
It moved me close to tears
When first I read
That you've been dead
For ninety million years.

Doug MacLeod

Over in the Meadow

Over in the meadow in the sand in the sun
Lived an old mother turtle and her little turtle — *one*.
'Dig,' said the mother. 'We dig,' said the one,
So they dug all day in the sand in the sun.

Over the meadow where the stream runs blue
Lived an old mother fish and her little fishes — *two*.
'Swim,' said the mother. 'We swim,' said the two,
So they swam all day where the stream runs blue.

Over in the meadow in a hole in a tree
Lived an old mother owl and her little owls — *three*.
'Tu-whoo,' said the mother. 'Tu-whoo,' said the three,
So they tu-whooed all day in a hole in a tree.

Over the meadow by the old barn door
Lived an old mother rat and her little
 ratties – *four*.
'Gnaw,' said the mother. 'We gnaw,' said
 the four,
So they gnawed all day by the old barn
 door.

Over in the meadow in a snug beehive
Lived an old mother bee and her little bees
 – *five*.
'Buzz,' said the mother. 'We buzz,' said the
 five,
So they buzzed all day in a snug beehive.

Over in the meadow in a nest built of sticks
Lived an old mother crow and her little
 crows – *six*.
'Caw,' said the mother. 'We caw,' said the
 six,
So they cawed all day in a nest built of
 sticks.

Over in the meadow where the grass grows
   so even
Lived an old mother frog and her little
   froggies – *seven*.
'Jump,' said the mother. 'We jump,' said the
   seven,
So they jumped all day where the grass
   grows so even.

Over in the meadow by the old mossy gate
Lived an old mother lizard and her little
   lizards – *eight*.
'Bask,' said the mother. 'We bask,' said the
   eight,
So they basked all day by the old mossy
   gate.

Over in the meadow by the old scotch pine
Lived an old mother duck and her little
   ducks – *nine*.
'Quack,' said the mother. 'We quack,' said
   the nine,
So they quacked all day by the old scotch
   pine.

Over in the meadow in a cosy wee den
Lived an old mother beaver and her little
    beavers – *ten*.
'Beave,' said the mother. 'We beave,' said
    the ten,
So they beaved all day in a cosy wee den.

Anon

As Soon as Fred Gets Out of Bed

As soon as Fred gets out of bed,
his underwear goes on his head.
His mother laughs, 'Don't put it there,
a head's no place for underwear!'
But near his ears, above his brains,
is where Fred's underwear remains.

At night when Fred goes back to bed,
he deftly plucks it off his head.
His mother switches off the light
and softly croons, 'Good night!
   Good night!'
And then for reasons no one knows,
Fred's underwear goes on his toes.

Jack Prelutsky

Ice Lolly

Red rocket
on a stick.
If it shines,
lick it quick.

Round the edges,
on the top,
round the bottom,
do not stop.

Suck the lolly
lick your lips.
Lick the sides
as it drips

off the stick –
quick, quick,
lick, lick –
Red rocket
on a stick.

Pie Corbett

As I Went Down Zig Zag

As I went down Zig Zag
The clock striking one,
I saw a man cooking
An egg in the sun.

> As I went down Zig Zag
> The clock striking two,
> I watched a man walk
> With one boot and one shoe.

As I went down Zig Zag
The clock striking three,
I heard a man murmuring
'Buzz!' like a bee.

> As I went down Zig Zag
> The clock striking four,
> I saw a man swim
> In no sea by shore.

As I went down Zig Zag
The clock striking five,
I caught a man keeping
A hog in a hive.

        As I went down Zig Zag
        The clock striking six,
        I met a man making
        A blanket of bricks.

As I went down Zig Zag
The clock striking seven,
A man asked me if
I was odd or was even.

        As I went down Zig Zag
        The clock striking eight,
        I saw a man sailing
        A seven-barred gate.

As I went down Zig Zag
The clock striking nine,
I saw a man milking
Where never were kine.

        As I went down Zig Zag
        The clock striking ten,
        I watched a man waltz
        With a cock and a hen.

As I went down Zig Zag
The clock striking eleven,
I saw a man baking
A loaf with no leaven.

        As I went down Zig Zag
        The clock striking twelve,
        For dyes from the rainbow
        I saw a man delve.

So if you'd keep your senses,
The point of my rhyme
Is don't go down Zig Zag
When the clocks start to chime.

Charles Causley

Zig Zag is the name of a steep footpath in Launceston, where the poet lives.

Moses

Moses supposes his toeses are roses,
But Moses supposes erroneously;
For nobody's toeses are posies of roses
As Moses supposes his toeses to be.

Anon

Round the Rugged Rock

Round and round the rugged rock
The ragged rascal ran,
How many R's are there in that?
Now tell me if you can.

Anon

Five Little Chickens

Said the first little chicken,
With a queer little squirm,
'Oh, I wish I could find
A fat little worm!'

Said the second little chicken,
With an odd little shrug,
'Oh, I wish I could find
A fat little bug!'

Said the third little chicken,
With a little sigh of grief,
'Oh, I wish I could find
A little green leaf!'

Said the fourth little chicken,
With a sharp little squeal,
'Oh, I wish I could find
Some nice yellow meal!'

Said the fifth little chicken,
With a faint little moan,
'I wish I could find
A wee gravel stone!'

'Now, see here,' said their mother
From the green garden patch,
'If you want any breakfast,
You must all come and scratch!'

Anon

Tailor

I saw a little Tailor sitting stitch, stitch,
  stitching
Cross-legged on the floor of his kitch, kitch,
  kitchen.
His thumbs and his fingers were so nim,
  nim, nimble
With his wax and his scissors and his thim,
  thim, thimble.

His silk and his cotton he was thread,
  thread, threading
For a gown and a coat for a wed, wed,
  wedding,
His needle flew as swift as a swal, swal,
  swallow,
And his spools and his reels had to fol, fol,
  follow.

He hummed as he worked a merry dit, dit,
  ditty:
'The Bride is as plump as she's pret, pret,
  pretty,

I wouldn't have her taller, or short, short,
    shorter,
She can laugh like the falling of wat, wat,
    water,

'She can put a cherry-pie, togeth, geth,
    gether,
She can dance as light as a feath, feath,
    feather,
She can sing as sweet as a fid, fid, fiddle,
And she's only twenty inches round the
    mid, mid, middle.'

The happy little Tailor went on stitch,
    stitch, stitching
The black and the white in his kitch, kitch,
    kitchen.
He will wear the black one, she will wear
    the white one,
And the knot the Parson ties will be a tight,
    tight, tight one.

Eleanor Farjeon

Two Witches

There was a witch
The witch had an itch
The itch was so itchy it
Gave her a twitch.

Another witch
Admired the twitch
So she started twitching
Though she had no itch.

Now both of them twitch
So it's hard to tell which
Witch has the itch and
Which witch has the twitch.

Alexander Resnikoff

My Heterodontosaurus

Sam's a Diplodocus fan, he loves their snaky
   necks.
My brother pins up pictures of
   Tyrannosaurus Rex.
There are horny ones and frilly ones and
   ones with knobbly scales
And ones I wouldn't like to meet with
   spikes upon their tails.
But of all the curious creatures in that far-
   fetched family
The Heterodontosaurus
   The Heterodontosaurus
      The Heterodontosaurus is the dinosaur
         for me.

My dinosaur's a dancer, she's nimble and she's neat
As she dances down to meet me on her dainty, birdy feet,
As she dances round to greet me with her cheeky, beaky grin,
And she gurgles when I tickle where she hasn't got a chin
And I feed her flower sandwiches and leaves fresh from the tree
Cos my Heterodontosaurus
  My Heterodontosaurus
    My Heterodontosaurus is the dinosaur for me.

And sometimes when she's very bored she likes a special treat
So she looks round the kitchen for anything that's sweet.
Then she'll swallow tubs of ice cream and cakes that Mum's just made
And waterfalls of strawberries and lakes of lemonade.
Last week she ate my brother's birthday smarties for her tea

Yes, my Heterodontosaurus
  My Heterodontosaurus
    My Heterodontosaurus is the dinosaur
      for me.

It isn't that she's greedy and I tell my mum
  and dad
That she's only being mischievous, she isn't
  really bad.
But Dad gets quite excited and his face goes
  cherry red,
He shouts 'Don't you know the dinosaur —
  the dinosaur is dead?'
Well, I know when grown-ups tell you
  things, they like you to agree
But still my Heterodontosaurus
  My Heterodontosaurus
    My Heterodontosaurus is the dinosaur
      for me.

They never will believe me and my brother
  thinks I'm mad,
My mum says I'll grow out of it and as for
  my old dad,
He yells at me 'You must have cotton wool
  between your ears
Because no one's seen a dinosaur for
  seventy million years!'
But I have got a dinosaur that no one else
  can see
It's my Heterodontosaurus
  My Heterodontosaurus
    My Heterodontosaurus is the dinosaur
      for me.

My dinosaur's a dancer, she's nimble and
  she's neat
As she dances down to meet me on her
  dainty, birdy feet,
As she dances round to greet me with her
  cheeky, beaky grin
And she gurgles when I tickle where she
  hasn't got a chin.
Yes, of all those curious creatures that ever
  used to be

The Heterodontosaurus
  The Heterodontosaurus
    The Heterodontosaurus is the dinosaur
      for me.

Leon Rosselson

Learner

Oh, Matilda, look at your Uncle Jim,
He's in the bathtub learning how to swim.
First he does the front stroke, then he does
  the side,
Now he's underwater swimming against
  the tide.

Anon

My Daddy Dances Tapstep

Roger's Daddy's clever
Daisy's flies a plane
Michael's does computers
And has a house in Spain.
Lucy's goes to London
He stays there every week . . .
    But my Daddy has an earring
        and lovely dancing feet.

He hasn't got a briefcase
He hasn't got a phone
He hasn't got a mortgage
And we haven't got a home.
He hasn't got a fax machine
We haven't got a car
    But he can dance and fiddle
        And my Daddy is
            A Star.

Peter Dixon

I Thought . . .

I thought it was
a hedgehog
but it was only
an old scrubbing brush
half-buried in the snow.

I thought it was
a blackbird
but it was only
some torn black plastic
caught in the branch of a tree.

I thought it was
a butterfly
but it was only
a scrap of paper
whirling about in the wind.

John Foster

The Three Little Kittens

Three little kittens lost their mittens;
And they began to cry,
  'Oh, mother dear,
  We very much fear
  That we have lost our mittens.'
'Lost your mittens!
You naughty kittens!
Then you shall have no pie!'
  'Mee-ow, mee-ow, mee-ow.'
'No, you shall have no pie.'
  'Mee-ow, mee-ow, mee-ow.'

The three little kittens found their mittens;
And they began to cry,
  'Oh mother dear,
  See here, see here!
  See, we have found our mittens!'
'Put on your mittens,
you silly kittens,
And you may have some pie.'
  'Purr-r, purr-r, purr-r,
  Oh, let us have the pie!
  Purr-r, purr-r, purr-r.'

The three little kittens put on their mittens,
And soon ate up the pie;
  'Oh, mother dear,
  We greatly fear
  That we have soiled our mittens!'
'Soiled your mittens!
You naughty kittens!'
Then they began to sigh,
  'Mee-ow, mee-ow, mee-ow.'
Then they began to sigh,
  'Mee-ow, mee-ow, mee-ow.'

The three little kittens washed their
  mittens,
And hung them out to dry;
  'Oh, mother dear,
  Do not you hear
  That we have washed our mittens?'
'Washed your mittens!
Oh, you're good kittens!
But I smell a rat close by,
Hush, hush! Mee-ow, mee-ow.'
  'We smell a rat close by,
  Mee-ow, mee-ow, mee-ow.'

Eliza Lee Follen

Bedtime

Five minutes, five minutes more, please!
   Let me stay five minutes more!
Can't I just finish the castle
   I'm building here on the floor?
Can't I just finish the story
   I'm reading here in my book?
Can't I just finish this bead-chain –
   It *almost* is finished, look!
Can't I just finish this game, please?
   When a game's once begun
It's a pity never to find out
   Whether you've lost or won.
Can't I just stay five minutes?
   Well, can't I stay just four?
Three minutes, then? two minutes?
   Can't I stay *one* minute more?

Eleanor Farjeon

I Am a Ghost Who's Lost His Boo

I am a ghost who's lost his boo,
my boo is gone from me,
and I'm without a single clue
to where my boo might be.
It makes me mope, it makes me pout,
it almost makes me moan,
a ghost is not a ghost without
a boo to call his own.

My boo was piercing, fierce, and loud,
I used to strut and boast,
for I was positively proud
to be a gruesome ghost.
But now that I'm without a boo,
I find it rather weird,
there's little for a ghost to do
whose boo has disappeared.

Although I hover here and there,
and haunt a hundred rooms,
it seems there's no one I can scare
unless my boo resumes.
I am a ghost who's lost his boo,
alas! A boo I lack,
if you should find my boo, then you
had better give it back.

Jack Prelutsky

Chums

He sits and begs; he gives a paw;
He is, as you can see,
The finest dog you ever saw,
And he belongs to me.

He follows everywhere I go
And even when I swim.
I laugh because he thinks, you know,
That I belong to him.

Arthur Guiterman

A Frog He Would A-Wooing Go

A Frog he would a-wooing go,
   Heigho, says Rowley,
Whether his mother would let him or no,
With a rowley, powley, gammon and
   spinach,
   Heigho, says Anthony Rowley!

So off he sets in his opera hat,
   Heigho, says Rowley,
And on the road he met with a rat,
With a rowley, powley, gammon and
   spinach,
   Heigho, says Anthony Rowley!

'Pray, Mr Rat, will you go with me,'
   Heigho, says Rowley,
'Kind Mrs Mousey for to see?'
With a rowley, powley, gammon and
   spinach,
   Heigho, says Anthony Rowley!

When they came to the door of Mousey's Hall,
Heigho, says Rowley,
They gave a loud knock, and they gave a loud call.
With a rowley, powley, gammon and spinach,
Heigho, says Anthony Rowley!

'Pray, Mrs Mouse, are you within?'
Heigho, says Rowley,
'Oh, yes, kind sirs, I'm sitting to spin.'
With a rowley, powley, gammon and spinach,
Heigho, says Anthony Rowley!

'Pray, Mrs Mouse, will you give us some beer?'
Heigho, says Rowley,
'For Froggy and I are fond of good cheer.'
With a rowley, powley, gammon and spinach,
Heigho, says Anthony Rowley!

'Pray, Mr Frog, will you give us a song?'
  Heigho, says Rowley,
'But let it be something that's not very long.'
With a rowley, powley, gammon and spinach,
  Heigho, says Anthony Rowley!

But while they were all a-merry-making,
  Heigho, says Rowley,
A cat and her kittens came tumbling in.
With a rowley, powley, gammon and spinach,
  Heigho, says Anthony Rowley.

The cat she seized the rat by the crown;
  Heigho, says Rowley,
The kittens they pulled the little mouse down.
With a rowley, powley, gammon and spinach,
  Heigho, says Anthony Rowley.

This put Mr Frog in a terrible fright,
Heigho, says Rowley,
He took up his hat, and wished them good night.
With a rowley, powley, gammon and spinach,
Heigho, says Anthony Rowley.

But as Froggy was crossing over a brook,
Heigho, says Rowley,
A lily-white duck came and swallowed him up.
With a rowley, powley, gammon and spinach,
Heigho, says Anthony Rowley.

Anon

The Furry Ones

I like –
the furry ones –
the waggy ones
the purry ones
the hoppy ones
that hurry,

the glossy ones
the saucy ones
the sleepy ones
the leapy ones
the mousy ones
that scurry,

the snuggly ones
the huggly ones
the never, never
ugly ones…
all soft
and warm
and furry.

Aileen Fisher

The Cupboard

I know a little cupboard,
With a teeny tiny key,
And there's a jar of Lollipops
For me, me, me.

It has a little shelf, my dear,
As dark as dark can be,
And there's a dish of Banbury Cakes
For me, me, me.

I have a small fat grandmamma
With a very slippery knee,
And she's Keeper of the Cupboard
With the key, key, key.

And when I'm very good, my dear,
As good as good can be
There's Banbury Cakes, and Lollipops
For me, me, me.

Walter de la Mare

As I Was Going to St Ives

As I was going to St Ives,
I met a man with seven wives;
Every wife had seven sacks;
Every sack had seven cats;
Every cat had seven kits.
Kits, cats, sacks, and wives –
How many were going to St Ives?

Anon

Answer: One. The others were coming *from* St Ives.

Finger-nails

Cut them on Monday,
   you cut them for health,
Cut them on Tuesday,
   you cut them for wealth,
Cut them on Wednesday,
   you cut them for news,
Cut them on Thursday,
   a new pair of shoes,
Cut them on Friday,
   you cut them for sorrow,
Cut them on Saturday,
   see your true love tomorrow,
Cut them on Sunday,
   ill luck will be with you all the week.

Anon

Wynken, Blynken, and Nod

Wynken, Blynken, and Nod one night
Sailed off in a wooden shoe –
Sailed on a river of crystal light,
Into a sea of dew.
'Where are you going, and what do you
   wish?'
The old moon asked the three.
'We have come to fish for the herring fish
That live in this beautiful sea;
Nets of silver and gold have we!'
>   Said Wynken,
>   Blynken,
>   And Nod.

The old moon laughed and sang a song,
As they rocked in the wooden shoe,
And the wind that sped them all night long
Ruffled the waves of dew.
The little stars were the herring fish
That lived in that beautiful sea –
'Now cast your nets wherever you wish –

Never afeared are we';
So cried the stars to the fishermen three:
    Said Wynken,
    Blynken,
    And Nod.

All night long their nets they threw
To the stars in the twinkling foam —
Then down from the skies came the wooden
  shoe,
Bringing the fishermen home;
'Twas all so pretty a sail it seemed
As if it could not be,
And some folks thought 'twas a dream
  they'd dreamed
Of sailing that beautiful sea —
But I shall name you the fishermen three:
    Said Wynken,
    Blynken,
    And Nod.

Wynken and Blynken are two little eyes,
And Nod is a little head,
And the wooden shoe that sailed the skies
Is a wee one's trundle-bed.
So shut your eyes while mother sings
Of wonderful sights that be,
And you shall see the beautiful things
As you rock in the misty sea,
Where the old shoe rocked the fishermen
   three:
       Said Wynken,
       Blynken,
       And Nod.

Eugene Field

Mice

Mice have a taste for bacon rind
Porridge oats and kippers
Remember this if you should find
Mice nesting in your slippers.

Miles Gibson

Deborah Delora

Deborah Delora, she liked a bit of fun –
She went to the baker's and she bought a penny bun;
Dipped the bun in treacle and threw it at her teacher –
Deborah Delora! what a wicked creature!

Anon

The Owl and the Pussy-Cat

The Owl and the Pussy-cat went to sea
  In a beautiful pea-green boat,
They took some honey, and plenty of
  money,
  Wrapped up in a five-pound note.
The Owl looked up to the stars above,
  And sang to a small guitar,
'O lovely Pussy! O Pussy, my love,
    What a beautiful Pussy you are,
      You are,
      You are!
    What a beautiful Pussy you are!'

  Pussy said to the Owl, 'You elegant fowl!
How charmingly sweet you sing!
O let us be married! too long we have
  tarried:
  But what shall we do for a ring?'
They sailed away, for a year and a day,
  To the land where the Bong-tree grows
And there in a wood a Piggy-wig stood

With a ring at the end of his nose,
   His nose,
   His nose,
With a ring at the end of his nose.

'Dear Pig, are you willing to sell for
  one shilling
  Your ring?' Said the Piggy, 'I will.'
So they took it away, and were married
  next day
  By the Turkey who lives on the hill.
They dined on mince, and slices of quince,
  Which they ate with a runcible spoon;
And hand in hand, on the edge of the sand,
   They danced by the light of the moon,
    The moon,
    The moon,
   They danced by the light of the moon.

Edward Lear

Cow

The Cow comes home swinging
Her udder and singing:

'The dirt O the dirt
It does me no hurt.

And a good splash of muck
Is a blessing of luck.

O I splosh through the mud
But the breath of my cud

Is sweeter than silk.
O I splush through manure

But my heart stays pure
As a pitcher of milk.'

Ted Hughes

Ready for Spaghetti

Pasta ribbons, pasta bows,
Pasta spirals, pasta Os,
Some is white and some is green,
Some comes with spinach in between.

It's shaped like tubes and wheels and strings
And named all sorts of funny things:
Ravioli, Tortellini,
Macaroni, and Linguini.

In my book it is supreme;
I like it best with peas and cream.
Pasta – there's no way to beat it.
The only thing to do is eat it!

Peggy Guthart

The Mouse, the Frog and the Little Red Hen

Once a Mouse, a Frog, and a Little
 Red Hen,
Together kept a house;
The Frog was the laziest of frogs,
And lazier still was the Mouse.

The work all fell on the Little Red Hen,
Who had to get the wood,
And build the fires, and scrub, and cook,
And sometimes hunt the food.

One day, as she went scratching round,
She found a bag of rye;
Said she, 'Now who will make some bread?'
Said the lazy Mouse, 'Not I.'

'Nor I,' croaked the Frog as he drowsed in
 the shade,
Red Hen made no reply,
But flew around with bowl and spoon,
And mixed and stirred the rye.

'Who'll make the fire to bake the bread?'
Said the Mouse again, 'Not I,'
And, scarcely op'ning his sleepy eyes,
Frog made the same reply.

The Little Red Hen said never a word,
But a roaring fire she made;
And while the bread was baking brown,
'Who'll set the table?' she said.

'Not I,' said the sleepy Frog with a yawn;
'Nor I,' said the Mouse again.
So the table she set and the bread put on,
'Who'll eat this bread?' said the Hen.

'I will!' cried the Frog. 'And I!' squeaked the
    Mouse,
As they near the table drew:
'Oh, no, you won't!' said the Little Red Hen,
And away with the loaf she flew.

Anon

Where Are You Going To?

'Where are you going to, my pretty maid?'
'I'm going a-milking, sir,' she said.

'May I go with you, my pretty maid?'
'You're kindly welcome, sir,' she said.

'What is your father, my pretty maid?'
'My father is a farmer, sir,' she said.

'What is your fortune, my pretty maid?'
'My face is my fortune, sir,' she said.

'Then I can't marry you, my pretty maid!'
'Nobody asked you, sir!' she said.

Anon

Toes in My Nose

I stuck my toes
In my nose
And I couldn't get them out.
I looked a little strange
And people began to shout,
'Why would you ever?
My goodness – I never!'
They got in a terrible snit.
It's simple, I said
As they put me to bed,
I just wanted to see
If they fit.

Sheree Fitch

Five Little Monkeys

Five little monkeys walked along the shore;
One went a-sailing,
Then there were four.
Four little monkeys climbed up a tree;
One of them tumbled down,
Then there were three.
Three little monkeys found a pot of glue;
One got stuck in it,
Then there were two.
Two little monkeys found a currant bun;
One ran away with it,
Then there was one.
One little monkey cried all afternoon,
So they put him in an aeroplane
And sent him to the moon.

Anon

Mumbling Bees

All around the garden flowers
Big velvet bees are bumbling,
They hover low and as they go
They're mumbling, mumbling, mumbling.

To lavender and snapdragons
The busy bees keep coming,
And all the busy afternoon
They're humming, humming, humming.

Inside each bell-shaped flower and rose
They busily go stumbling,
Collecting pollen all day long
And bumbling, bumbling, bumbling.

Daphne Lister

The North Wind Doth Blow

The north wind doth blow,
And we shall have snow,
And what will the robin do then,
    poor thing?
  He'll sit in a barn,
  And keep himself warm,
And hide his head under his wing,
    poor thing!

The north wind doth blow,
And we shall have snow,
And what will the swallow do then,
    poor thing?
  Oh, do you not know
  That he's off long ago,
To a country where he will find spring,
    poor thing!

The north wind doth blow,
And we shall have snow,
And what will the dormouse do then,
    poor thing?
  Roll'd up like a ball,
  In his nest snug and small,
He'll sleep till warm weather comes in,
    poor thing!

The north wind doth blow,
And we shall have snow,
And what will the honey-bee do then,
    poor thing?
  In his hive he will stay
  Till the cold is away,
And then he'll come out in the spring,
    poor thing!

The north wind doth blow,
And we shall have snow,
And what will the children do then,
    poor things?
  When lessons are done,
   They must skip, jump and run,
Until they have made themselves warm,
    poor things!

Anon

A Rabbit Raced a Turtle

A rabbit raced a turtle,
You know the turtle won;
And Mister Bunny came in late,
A little hot cross bun!

Anon

Riddle

I am . . .
  spiral.
    Twisting shell
      on velvet black;
        track of silver,
          glider-one-foot,
         home on back.
          Leaf-feast hunter,
            stalk-eyes high
              above the leaf-feast trail.
                What am I . . . ?

Judith Nicholls

Answer: A snail.

One, Two, Three, Four, Five

One, two, three, four, five,
Once I caught a fish alive,
Six, seven, eight, nine, ten,
Then I let it go again.

Why did you let it go?
Because it bit my finger so.
Which finger did it bite?
This little finger on the right.

Anon

Mother Duck

Old Mother Duck has hatched a brood
Of ducklings, small and callow;
Their little wings are short, their down
Is mottled, grey and yellow.

There is a quiet little stream
That runs into the moat,
Where tall green sedges spread their leaves,
And water-lilies float.

Close by the margin of the brook
The old duck made her nest,
Of straw, and leaves, and withered grass,
And down from her own breast.

And there she sat for four long weeks,
In rainy days and fine,
Until the ducklings all came out –
Four, five, six, seven, eight, nine.

One peeped out from beneath her wing,
One scrambled on her back;
'That's very rude,' said Old Dame Duck,
'Get off! quack, quack, quack, quack!'

Anon

The Picnic

We brought a rug for sitting on,
Our lunch was in a box.
The sand was warm. We didn't wear
Hats or Shoes or Socks.

Waves came curling up the beach.
We waded. It was fun.
Our sandwiches were different kinds.
I dropped my jelly one.

Dorothy Aldis

How to be Angry

Scrunch your eyebrows
up to your hair,
pull on your chin
and glare glare glare,

puff out your cheeks,
puff puff puff,
then take a deep breath
and huff huff huff.

Eve Merriam

Sneezing

Sneeze on Monday, sneeze for danger;
Sneeze on Tuesday, kiss a stranger;
Sneeze on Wednesday, get a letter;
Sneeze on Thursday, something better;
Sneeze on Friday, sneeze for sorrow;
Sneeze on Saturday, joy tomorrow.

Anon

There was a Young Girl

There was a young girl of Asturias,
Whose temper was frantic and furious.
   She used to throw eggs
   At her grandmother's legs –
A habit unpleasant, but curious.

Anon

Jelly Jake and Butter Bill

Jelly Jake and Butter Bill
One dark night when all was still
Pattered down the long, dark stair,
And no one saw the guilty pair;
Pushed aside the pantry-door
And there found everything galore, –
Honey, raisins, orange-peel,
Cold chicken aplenty for a meal,
Gingerbread enough to fill
Two such boys as Jake and Bill.
Well, they ate and ate and ate,
Gobbled at an awful rate
Till I'm sure they soon weighed more
Than double what they did before.
And then, it's awful, still it's true,
The floor gave way and they went through.
Filled so full they couldn't fight,
Slowly they sank out of sight.
Father, Mother, Cousin Ann,
Cook and nurse and furnace man
Fished in forty-dozen ways
After them, for twenty days;

But not a soul has chanced to get
A glimpse or glimmer of them yet.
And I'm afraid we never will –
Poor Jelly Jake and Butter Bill.

Leroy F. Jackson

Maggie

There was a small maiden named Maggie,
Whose dog was enormous and shaggy;
   The front end of him
     Looked vicious and grim –
But the tail end was friendly and waggy.

Anon

The Cat's Pyjamas

*This bedroom looks like
there's been an earthquake!
Tidy everything away, right now.*

I can't, Mum.
It's Wizard Wondro's Infernal Castle Trap
for melting mean monsters.
You're standing in it.

*And put the tops on those felt tip pens.
They'll go dry.*

They're ray guns to scorch beams of light
across the path of enemies
who approach the drawbridge.

*Isn't that your homework book?
Pick it up from the rug.*

It's a secret coded message from Wizard
 Wondro
to guide his followers
across the evil swamp.

*I suppose those are Wizard Windro's pyjamas.
Put them in the drawer.*

They're not Wizard Wondro's.
He wears invisible magic armour,
proof against all weapons
yet light enough to fly in.

Then whose pyjamas are they?

Er . . . I expect they belong to the cat.

Irene Rawnsley

The Elf and the Dormouse

Under a toadstool crept a wee elf,
Out of the rain, to shelter himself.

Under the toadstool, sound asleep,
Sat a big dormouse all in a heap.

Trembled the wee elf, frightened, and yet
Fearing to fly away lest he get wet.

To the next shelter — maybe a mile!
Sudden the wee elf smiled a wee smile,

Tugged till the toadstool toppled in two,
Holding it over him, gaily he flew.

Soon he was safe home, dry as could be,
Soon woke the dormouse — 'Good gracious me!

Where is my toadstool?' loud he lamented.
And that's how umbrellas first were invented.

Oliver Herford

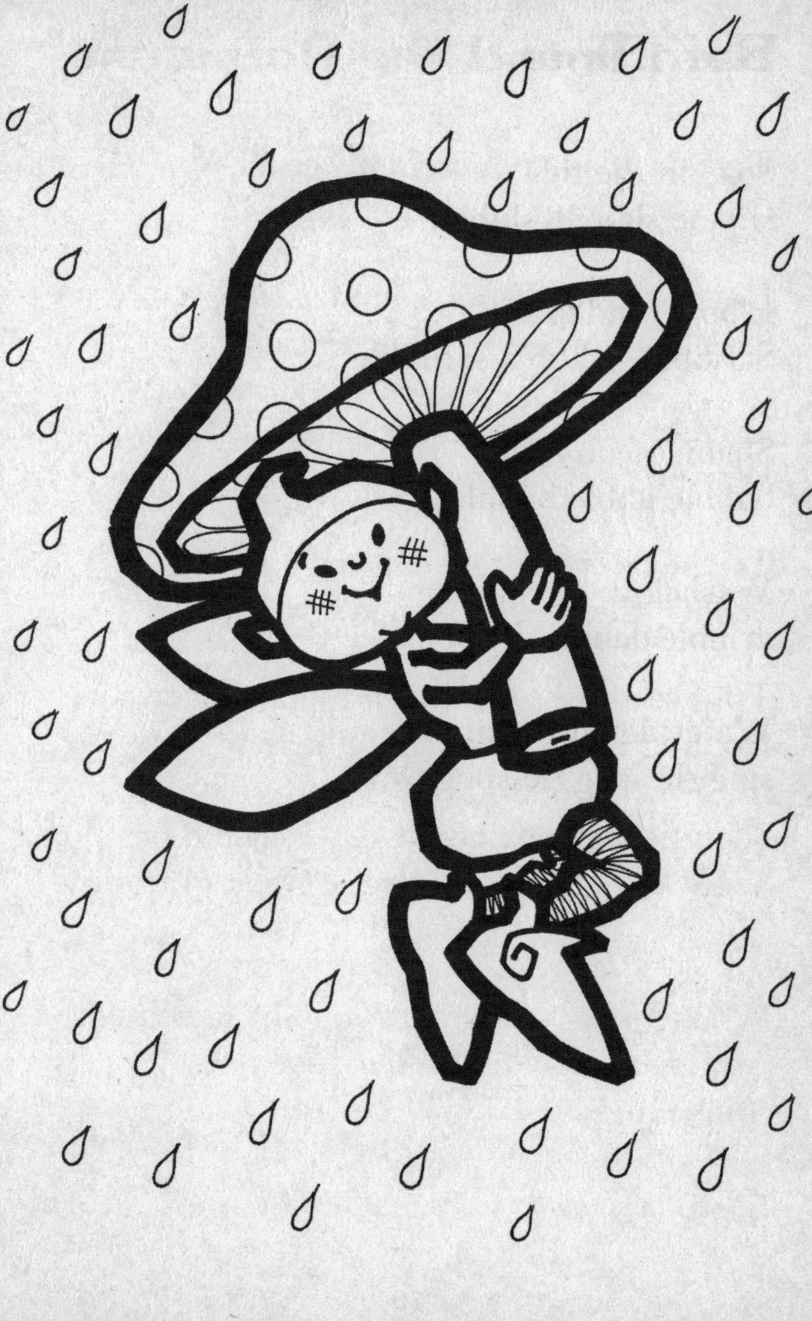

Bath Time

Soap in the tub
slipple slapple slubble

Elbows and knees
Scribble scrabble scrubble

Shampoo on head
bubble ubble bubble

Washcloth to squeeze
dribble dabble drubble

Water down the drain
spiggle spaggle spuggle

Water nearly gone
guggle uggle gluggle

Gurgle
   urgle
      gug

Eve Merriam

Simple Simon

Simple Simon met a pieman,
Going to the fair;
Says Simple Simon to the pieman,
'Let me taste your ware.'

Says the pieman to Simple Simon,
'Show me first your penny,'
Says Simple Simon to the pieman,
'Indeed I have not any.'

Simple Simon went a-fishing
For to catch a whale;
All the water he could find
Was in his mother's pail!

Simple Simon went to look
If plums grew on a thistle;
He pricked his fingers very much,
Which made poor Simon whistle.

He went to catch a dicky bird,
And thought he could not fail,
Because he had a little salt,
To put upon its tail.

He went for water with a sieve,
But soon it ran all through;
And now poor Simple Simon
Bids you all adieu.

Anon

Three Ghostesses

Three little ghostesses,
Sitting on postesses,
Eating buttered toastesses,
Greasing their fistesses,
Up to their wristesses,
Oh, what beastesses
To make such feastesses!

Anon

The Clucking Hen

'Will you take a walk with me,
My little wife, today?
There's barley in the barley field,
And hayseed in the hay.'

'Thank you,' said the clucking hen.
'I've something else to do;
I'm busy sitting on my eggs,
I cannot walk with you.'

The clucking hen sat on her nest,
She made it on the hay;
And warm and snug beneath her breast
A dozen white eggs lay.

CRACK! CRACK! went all the eggs,
Out dropped the chickens small.
'Cluck!' said the clucking hen.
'Now I have you all.

Come along, my little chicks,
I'll take a walk with you.'
'Hello!' said the rooster.
'Cock-a-doodle-doo!'

Anon

Pease Porridge

Pease porridge hot,
Pease porridge cold,
Pease porridge in the pot,
Nine days old.

Some like it hot,
Some like it cold,
Some like it in the pot,
Nine days old.

Anon

Captain Conniption

I'm Captain Conniption,
the scourge of the sea,
no pirate alive
is as fearsome as me,
I'm ten times as tough
as the skin of a whale,
the sharks cringe in terror
wherever I sail.

I'm Captain Conniption,
the bane of the fleet,
I don't wash my face,
and I don't wash my feet,
I wear a black hat
and I fly a black flag,
I'm bad as can be,
though I don't like to brag.

When I'm on the deck
with my cutlass in hand,
the saltiest sailors
start sailing for land,
they know I'm the nastiest
nautical knave,
and bold as a brigand
is bound to behave.

I'm Captain Conniption,
and up to no good,
you'll soon walk the plank
if I think that you should,
I'd show you right now
how I vanquish a foe,
but I hear my mother,
so I have to go.

Jack Prelutsky

Muddy Boots

Trudging down the country lane,
Splodgely thlodgely plooph,
Two foot deep in slimy mud.
Falomph Polopf Galloph.
Hopolosplodgely go your boots,
Splothopy gruthalamie golumph.
Then you find firm ground again,
Plonky shlonky clonky.
BUT . . . then you sink back in again,
Squelchy crathpally hodgle.

Sitting outside scraping your boots,
Scalpey gulapy criketty,
Cursing the horrible six inch slodge,
Scrapey flakey cakey.
Flakes of mud, crispling off the boots,
Crinkey splinky schlinkle.
Never again, will I venture into that
... Schlodgely, Flopchely, Thlodgely,
   schrinkshely,
      slimy,
         grimy,
            squelchy,
              ghastly
MUD!

Philip Paddon

Mr Finney's Turnip

Mr Finney had a turnip
And it grew behind the barn
And it grew and it grew,
And that turnip did no harm.

There it grew and it grew
Till it could grow no longer;
Then his daughter Lizzie picked it
And put it in the cellar.

There it lay and it lay
Till it began to rot;
And his daughter Susie took it
And put it in the pot.

And they boiled it and boiled it
As long as they were able;
And then his daughters took it
And put it on the table.

Mr Finney and his wife
They sat them down to sup;
And they ate and they ate
And they ate that turnip up.

Anon

Granny, Granny, Please Comb My Hair

Granny Granny please comb
my hair
you always take your time
you always take such care

You put me on a cushion
between your knees
you rub a little coconut oil
parting gentle as a breeze

Mummy Mummy
she's always in a hurry-hurry
rush
she pulls my hair
sometimes she tugs

But Granny
you have all the time
in the world
and when you're finished
you always turn my head and say
'Now who's a nice girl?'

Grace Nichols

Night, Knight

'Night, night,'
said one knight
to the other knight
the other night.
'Night, night, knight.'

Anon

My Gran

My Gran is
    a giggle-in-the-corner-like-a-child
        kind of Gran

She is
    a put-your-cold-hand-in-my-pocket
    a keep-your-baby-curls-in-my-locket
        kind of Gran
She is
    a make-it-better-with-a-treacle-toffee
    a what-you-need's-a-cup-of-milky-coffee
    a hurry-home-I-love-you-awfully
        kind of Gran

She is
    a butter-ball-for-your-bad-throat
    a stitch-your-doll-a-new-green-coat
    a let's-make-soapy-bubbles-float
    a hold-my-hand-I'm-seasick-in-a-boat
        kind of Gran

She is
>   a toast-your-tootsies-by-the-fire
>   a crack-the-wishbone-for-your-heart's-
>   desire
>   a ladies-don't-sweat-they-perspire
>   a funny-old-fashioned-higgledy-
>   piggledy-lady-to-admire
>   kind of Gran

And this lovely grandmother
>   is mine, all mine!

Moira Andrew

Give Me a House

Give me a house, said Polly.
Give me land, said Hugh.
Give me the moon, said Sadie.
Give me the sun, said Sue.

Give me a horse, said Rollo.
Give me a hound, said Joe.
Give me fine linen, said Sarah.
Give me silk, said Flo.

Give me a mountain, said Kirsty.
Give me a valley, said Jim.
Give me a river, said Dodo.
Give me the sky, said Tim.

Give me the ocean, said Adam.
Give me a ship, said Hal.
Give me a kingdom, said Rory.
Give me a crown, said Sal.

Give me gold, said Peter.
Give me silver, said Paul.
Give me love, said Jenny,
Or nothing at all.

Charles Causley

There was a Little Girl

There was a little girl
And she had a little curl
Right in the middle of her forehead.
When she was good
She was very very good,
But when she was bad she was horrid.

Anon

The Gingerbread Man

The gingerbread man gave a gingery shout:
'Quick! Open the oven and let me out!'
He stood up straight in his baking pan.
He jumped to the floor and away he ran.
'Catch me,' he called, 'if you can, can, can.'

The gingerbread man met a cock and a pig
And a dog that was brown and twice as big
As himself. But he called to them all as he
　　ran,
'You can't catch a runaway gingerbread
　　man.'

The gingerbread man met a reaper and
　　sower.
The gingerbread man met a thresher
　　and mower;
But no matter how fast they scampered
　　and ran,
They couldn't catch up with the
　　gingerbread man.

Then he came to a fox and he turned to face him.
He dared Old Reynard to follow and chase him;
But when he stopped under the fox's nose
Something happened. What do you suppose?
The fox gave a snap. The fox gave a yawn,
And the gingerbread man was gone, gone, GONE.

Rowena Bennett

Breakfast for One

Hot thick crusty buttery toast
Buttery toasty thick hot crust
Crusty buttery hot thick toast
Crusty thick hot toasty butter
Thick hot buttery crusty toast
Toasty buttery hot thick crust
Hot buttery thick crusty toast —

With marmalade is how I like it most!

Judith Nicholls

Be Kind to Dumb Animals

There once was an ape in a zoo
Who looked out through the bars and saw —
    YOU!
    Do you think it's fair
    To give poor apes a scare?
I think it's a mean thing to do!

John Ciardi

What I'll Do To Make You Laugh

I'll ho-ho-ho and I'll chuck-chuck-chuckle.
I'll tee-hee-hee and I'll yuck-yuck-yuckle.
I'll hardy-har-har, and when I'm through,
If you're not laughing, I'll boo-hoo-hoo!

Jeff Moss

I'm Not Frightened of Pussy Cats

I'm not frightened of Pussy Cats,
They only eat up mice and rats,
But a Hippopotamus
Could eat the Lotofus!

Spike Milligan

My Name Is

My name is Sluggery-wuggery
My name is Worms-for-tea
My name is Swallow-the-table-leg
My name is Drink-the-Sea.

My name is I-eat-Saucepans
My name is I-like-snails
My name is Grand-Piano-George
My name is I-ride-whales.

My name is Jump-the-chimney
My name is Bite-my-knee
My name is Jiggery-pokery
And Riddle-me-ree, and ME.

Pauline Clarke

Little Bo-Peep

Little Bo-Peep has lost her sheep,
And can't tell where to find them;
Leave them alone, and they will come home,
Bringing their tails behind them.

Anon

Not a Very Cheerful Song, I'm Afraid

There was a gloomy lady,
With a gloomy duck and a gloomy drake,
And they all three wandered gloomily,
Beside a gloomy lake,
On a gloomy, gloomy, gloomy, gloomy,
gloomy, gloomy day.

Now underneath that gloomy lake
The gloomy lady's gone.
But the gloomy duck and the gloomy drake
Swim on and on and on,
On a gloomy, gloomy, gloomy, gloomy,
gloomy, gloomy day.

Adrian Mitchell

Grandma's Lullaby

Close your eyes,
My precious love,
Grandma's little
Turtledove.

Go to sleep now,
Pretty kitty,
Grandma's little
Chickabiddy.

Stop your crying,
Cuddly cutie,
Grandma's little
Sweet patootie.

Issum, wissum,
Popsy wopsy,
Tootsie wootsie
Lollypopsie
Diddims
Huggle
Snuggle pup

And now, for Grandma's sake, hush up!

Charlotte Pomerantz

Tiger, Tiger

The tiger that stalks through the night
Delivers a hideous bite
And there on his paws
Are hideous claws
But apart from all that, he's all right!

Pam Ayres

Countdown

There are ten ghosts in the pantry,
There are nine upon the stairs,
There are eight ghosts in the attic,
There are seven on the chairs,
There are six within the kitchen,
There are five along the hall,
There are four upon the ceiling,
There are three upon the wall,
There are two ghosts on the carpet,
Doing things that ghosts will do,
There is one ghost right behind me
Who is oh so quiet . . . BOO.

Jack Prelutsky

Bears Don't Like Bananas

Monkeys like to play the drums,
    badgers wear bandannas.
Tigers like to tickle toes
    but bears don't like bananas.

A crocodile can juggle buns
    on visits to his nana's.
Seagulls like to dance and sing
    but bears don't like bananas.

Rats and mice can somersault
    and do gymnastics with iguanas.
Weasels like to wiggle legs
    but bears don't like bananas.

A porcupine likes drinking tea,
    and cheering at gymkhanas.
A ladybird likes eating pies
    but bears don't like bananas.

John Rice

I Speak, I Say, I Talk

Cats purr.
Lions roar.
Owls hoot.
Bears snore.
Crickets creak.
Mice squeak.
Sheep baa.
But I SPEAK!

Monkeys chatter.
Cows moo.
Ducks quack.
Doves coo.
Pigs squeal.
Horses neigh.
Chickens cluck.
But I SAY!

Flies hum
Dogs growl.
Bats screech.
Coyotes howl.
Frogs croak.
Parrots squawk.
Bees buzz.
But I TALK!

Arnold L. Shapiro

My Brother
is as Generous
as Anyone Could Be

My brother is as generous
as anyone could be,
for everything he's ever had
he's always shared with me.
He has loaned me his binoculars,
his new computer games,
and his wind-up walking dragon
that breathes artificial flames.

I've been grateful for his robots,
for his giant teddy bear,
but not for certain other things
I'd hoped he'd never share –
Though I'm glad he's shared his rockets
and his magic jumping rocks,
I wish my brother hadn't shared
his case of chicken-pox.

Jack Prelutsky

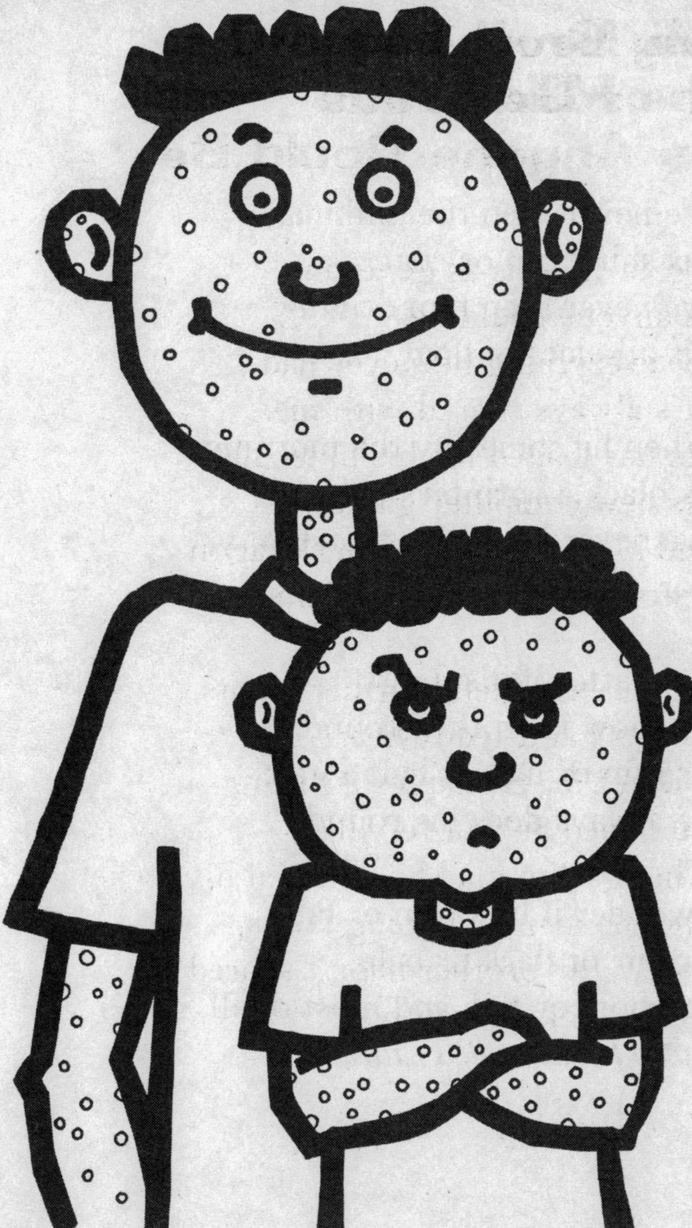

I've Never Seen the Milkman

I've never seen the milkman,
His shiny cap or coat.
I've never seen him driving
His all-electric float.

When he comes by the morning's
As black as printers' ink
I've never heard his footstep
Nor a single bottle clink.

No matter if it's foggy
Or snow is on the ground,
Or rain or hail or half a gale
He always does his round.

I wonder if he's thin or fat
Or fair or dark or bald,
Or short or tall, and most of all
I wonder what he's called.

He goes to bed so early
That not an owl has stirred,
And rises up again before
The earliest early bird.

God bless the faithful milkman,
My hero — and that's flat!
Or perhaps he's a milklady?
(I've never thought of that.)

Charles Causley

Hickory, Dickory, Dock

Hickory, Dickory, Dock,
The mouse ran down the clock –
She had watched the cat go out of the door,
She saw some crumbs on the kitchen floor,
And she gobbled them up – Tick-tock!

Hickory, Dickory, Dock,
The mouse ran up the clock –
For she heard the stealthy tread of the cat,
And she didn't care to stay after that,
So she scampered back – Tick-tock!

Hickory, Dickory, Dock,
The mouse slept in the clock –
But when she awoke, she gnawed her way
Through the old clock-case one winter day,
And never came back – Tick-tock!

Anon

Wild Beasts

I will be a lion
    And you shall be a bear,
And each of us will have a den
    Beneath a nursery chair;
And you must growl and growl and growl,
    And I will roar and roar,
And then – why, then – you'll growl again,
    And I will roar some more!

Evaleen Stein

Through the Teeth

Through the teeth
Past the gums
Look out, stomach
Here it comes!

Anon

Clatter

If I should list my favourite words,
They'd sound a lot like this:
Rumble, crash, snort, jangle, thump,
Roar, fizzle, splat, moo, hiss.
Not to mention gobble, clang,
Tweet, sputter, ticktock, growl;
Crackle, chirp, boom, whistle, wheeze,
Squawk, jingle, quack, thud, howl.
Then of course there's grunt, toot, cuckoo,
Thunder, bang, pop, mush,
Rattle, splash, rip, ding-dong, and . . .
My parents' favourite — *Hush!*

Joyce Armor

Quack, Quack!

We have two ducks. One blue. One black.
And when our blue duck goes 'Quack-quack'
our black duck quickly quack-quacks back.
The quacks Blue quacks make her quite a
  quacker
but Black is a quicker quacker-backer.

Dr Seuss

be be be quiet

be be be quiet
in assembly
be be be loud in
the playground
be be be good in school
be be be bad in your
dreams

Mark Warren (aged 5)

A Cough

I have a little cough, sir,
In my little chest, sir,
Every time I cough, sir,
It leaves a little pain, sir,
Cough, cough, cough, cough,
There it is again, sir.

Robert Graves

Some Things Don't Make Any Sense At All

My mom says I'm her sugarplum.
My mom says I'm her lamb.
My mom says I'm completely perfect
Just the way I am.
My mom says I'm a super-special wonderful
terrific little guy
My mom just had another baby.
Why?

Judith Viorst

The Pancake

Mix a pancake,
Stir a pancake,
    Pop it in the pan;
Fry the pancake,
Toss the pancake –
    Catch it if you can!

Christina Rossetti

The Mouse

I heard a mouse
Bitterly complaining
In a crack of moonlight
Aslant on the floor.

'Little I ask
And that little is not granted.
There are very few crumbs
In the world any more.

'The Bread box is tin
And I cannot get in.

'The jam's in a jar
My teeth cannot mar.

'The cheese sits by itself
On the pantry shelf.

'All night I run
Searching and seeking,
All night I run
About on the floor.

'Moonlight is there
And a bare place for dancing,
But no little feast
Is spread any more.'

Elizabeth Coatsworth

Monday's Child

Monday's child is fair of face,
Tuesday's child is full of grace,
Wednesday's child is full of woe,
Thursday's child has far to go,
Friday's child is loving and giving,
Saturday's child works hard for a living,
And the child that is born on the Sabbath
　day
Is bonny and blithe, and good and gay.

Anon

Rolling Down a Hill

I'm rolling
rolling
rolling
down

I'm rolling
down a
hill.

I'm rolling
rolling
rolling
down

I'm rolling
down it
still.

I'm rolling
rolling
rolling
down

I'm rolling
down a
hill

I'm rolling
rolling
rolling
down

But now
I'm feeling
ill.

Colin West

A Wise Old Owl

A wise old owl lived in an oak;
The more he saw the less he spoke;
The less he spoke the more he heard.
Why can't we be like that wise old bird?

Anon

Acknowledgements

The compiler and publishers wish to thank the following for permission to use copyright material:

Dorothy Aldis, 'The Picnic' from *All Together* by Dorothy Aldis. Copyright , 1925-1928, 1934, 1939, 1952, renewed 1953, 1954-1956, 1962 by Dorothy Aldis, Copyright © 1967 by Roy E Porter, renewed, by permission of G P Putnam's Sons, a division of Penguin Putnam Inc; **Moira Andrew**, 'My Gran', first published in *Unzip Your Lips*, edited by Paul Cookson, Macmillan (1998). Copyright © Moira Andrew, by permission of the author; **Pam Ayres**, 'Tiger, Tiger' from *The Works: Selected Poems* by Pam Ayres. Copyright © Pam Ayres 1992, by permission of BBC Worldwide Ltd.; **Charles Causley**, 'As I Went Down Zig-Zag', 'I've Never Seen the Milkman' and 'Give Me a House' from *Collected Poems for Children* by Charles Causley, Macmillan, by permission of David Higham Associates on behalf of the author; **Pauline Clarke**, 'My Name is ...' from *Silver Bells and Cockle Shells* by Pauline Clarke. Copyright © Pauline Clarke 1962, by permission of Curtis Brown, London on behalf of the author; **Elizabeth Coatsworth**, 'The Mouse' from *Compass Rose* by Elizabeth Coatsworth. Copyright © 1929 by Coward-McCann, Inc, renewed Copyright © 1957 by Elizabeth Coatsworth, by permission of Coward-McCann, Inc, a division of Penguin-Putnam Inc; **Pie Corbett**, 'Ice Lolly', first published in *Another Very First Poetry Book*, ed. John Foster, Oxford University Press. Copyright © 1992 by Pie Corbett, by permission of the author; **Peter Dixon**, 'My Daddy Dances Tapstep' from *Peter Dixon's Grand Prix of Poetry*, Macmillan, by permission of the author; **Aileen Fisher**, 'The Furry Ones' from *Feathered Ones and Furry* by Aileen Fisher. Copyright © 1971, 1995 Aileen Fisher, by permission of Marian Reiner on behalf of the author; **Eleanor Farjeon**, 'Bedtime' and 'Tailor' from *Blackbird Has Spoken* by Eleanor Farjeon, by permission of David Higham Associates on behalf of the author; **Sheree Fitch**, 'Toes in My Nose' from *Toes in My Nose* by Sheree Fitch (1987), by permission of Doubleday Canada; **John Foster**, 'I thought ...', first published in *My Violet Poetry Book*, ed. Moira Andrew, Macmillan. Copyright © 1988 John Foster, by permission of the author; **Miles Gibson**, 'Mice' from *Say Hello to the Buffalo* by Miles Gibson, Heinemann. Copyright © 1994 Miles Gibson, by permission of Jonathan Clowes Ltd on behalf of the author; **Robert Graves**, 'The Cough' from *Complete Poems* by Robert Graves, by permission of Carcanet Press Ltd; **Ted Hughes**, 'Cow' from *The Cat and the Cuckoo* by Ted Hughes, by permission of Faber and Faber Ltd; **Leroy F. Jackson**, 'Jelly Jake and Butter Bill' from *Beastly Boys and Ghastly Girls*, ed. William Cole, by permission of Laurence Pollinger on behalf of William Cole; **Daphne Lister**, 'Mumbling Bees', by permission of the author; **Walter de la Mare**, 'Some One', 'The Ride-by-Nights' and 'The Cupboard' from *The Complete Poems of Walter* *de la Mare* (1969), by permission of The Society of Authors as the Literary Trustees of Walter de la Mare; **Doug Macleod**, 'Ode to an Extinct Dinosaur' from *The Garden of Bad Things*, by permission of Penguin Books Australia Ltd; **Eve Merriam**, 'Bath Time' and' How to be Angry' from *Higgle Wiggle* by Eve Merriam, Morrow Junior Books/HarperCollins. Copyright © 1994 Estate of Eve Merriam, by permission of Marian Reiner on behalf of the Estate of the author; **Adrian Mitchell**, 'Not a Very Cheerful Song, I'm Afraid' from *Blue Lagoon and the Magic Islands of Poetry* by Adrian Mitchell, Orchard Books. Copyright © 1997 Adrian Mitchell, by permission of Peters Fraser & Dunlop Group Ltd on behalf of the author; **Spike Milligan**, 'I'm Not Frightened of Pussy Cats', by permission of Spike Milligan Productions Ltd; **Jeff Moss**, 'What I'll Do to Make You Laugh' from *The Other Side of the Door*, by permission of ICM, Inc on behalf of the author; **Judith Nicholls**, 'Riddle'. Copyright © 1990 Judith Nicholls, and 'Breakfast for One'. Copyright © 1986 Judith Nicholls, by permission of the author; **Grace Nichols**, 'Granny, Granny, Please Comb my Hair' from *Come On Into My Tropical Garden*, A & C Black. Copyright © 1988 by Grace Nichols, by permission of Curtis Brown Ltd, London, on behalf of the author; **Jack Prelutsky**, 'As Soon as Fred Gets Out of Bed', 'I Am a Ghost Who's Lost His Boo', 'My Brother is as Generous as Anyone Can Be' and 'Captain Conniption' from *Something Big Has Been Here* by Jack Prelutsky, Heinemann Young Books. Copyright © Jack Prelutsky 1990; and 'Countdown' from *It's Halloween*, World's Work Ltd. Copyright © Jack Prelutsky 1977, by permission of Egmont Children's Books Ltd; **Irene Rawnsley**, 'The Cat's Pyjamas' from *House of a Hundred Cats* by Irene Rawnsley, Methuen (1995), by permission of the author; **John Rice**, 'Bears Don't Like Bananas', by permission of the author; **Leon Rosselson**, 'My Hetorodontosaurus'. Copyright © Leon Rosselson, by permission of David Highan Associates on behalf of the author; **Dr Seuss**, 'Quack, Quack' from *Oh Say Can You Say* by Dr Seuss. Copyright © by Dr Seuss Enterprises, L.P. 1979, by permission of Random House Children's Books, a division of Random House, Inc and HarperCollins Publishers Ltd; **Judith Viorst**, 'Some Things Don't Make Any Sense At All' from *If I Were in Charge of the World and Other Worries* (1981). Copyright © Judith Viorst 1981, by permission of A M Heath on behalf of the author and Atheneum Books for Young Readers, an imprint of Simon & Schuster Children's Publishing Division; **Mark Warren**, 'be be be quiet' from *Young Words*, Young Writers Competition, Macmillan/W H Smith (1993), by permission of W H Smith; **Colin West**, 'Rolling Down a Hill' from *The Best of West*, Hutchinson (1990), by permission of the author;

Every effort has been made to trace the copyright holders but where this has not been possible or where any error has been made the publishers will be pleased to make the necessary arrangement at the first opportunity.